1 MONTH OF FREE READING

at
www.ForgottenBooks.com

By purchasing this book you are eligible for one month membership to ForgottenBooks.com, giving you unlimited access to our entire collection of over 1,000,000 titles via our web site and mobile apps.

To claim your free month visit: www.forgottenbooks.com/free231943

* Offer is valid for 45 days from date of purchase. Terms and conditions apply.

ISBN 978-1-5285-6075-7
PIBN 10231943

This book is a reproduction of an important historical work. Forgotten Books uses state-of-the-art technology to digitally reconstruct the work, preserving the original format whilst repairing imperfections present in the aged copy. In rare cases, an imperfection in the original, such as a blemish or missing page, may be replicated in our edition. We do, however, repair the vast majority of imperfections successfully; any imperfections that remain are intentionally left to preserve the state of such historical works.

Forgotten Books is a registered trademark of FB &c Ltd.
Copyright © 2018 FB &c Ltd.
FB &c Ltd, Dalton House, 60 Windsor Avenue, London, SW19 2RR.
Company number 08720141. Registered in England and Wales.

For support please visit www.forgottenbooks.com

THE LITTLE AUGUSTINE LEARNS TO KNOW JESUS CHRIST.

Frontispiece.

AINT MONICA

BY

F. A. FORBES

WITH THREE ORIGINAL ILLUSTRATIONS BY
FRANK ROSS MAGUIRE

SECOND EDITION

CONTENTS

CHAPTER PAGE

I. HOW ST. MONICA WAS BROUGHT UP BY CHRISTIAN PARENTS IN THE CITY OF TAGASTE 13

II. HOW ST. MONICA LIVED IN THE PAGAN HOUSEHOLD OF HER HUSBAND PATRICIUS 23

III. HOW ST. MONICA BROUGHT UP HER CHILDREN, AND HOW THE LITTLE AUGUSTINE FELL SICK AND DESIRED BAPTISM 33

IV. HOW ST. MONICA BY HER GENTLENESS AND CHARITY WON PATRICIUS AND HIS

CONTENTS

	PAGE
HOW AUGUSTINE PLANNED TO GO TO ROME, AND HOW HE CRUELLY DECEIVED HIS MOTHER	84
HOW AUGUSTINE CAME TO MILAN, AND HOW HIS TEMPEST-TOSSED SOUL FOUND LIGHT AND PEACE AT LAST	94
HOW ST. MONICA LIVED AT CASSIACUM WITH AUGUSTINE AND HIS FRIENDS, AND HOW AUGUSTINE WAS BAPTIZED BY ST. AMBROSE	107
HOW ST. MONICA SET OUT FOR AFRICA WITH ST. AUGUSTINE, AND HOW SHE DIED AT OSTIA ON THE TIBER	118

ILLUSTRATIONS

FACING PAGE

THE LITTLE AUGUSTINE LEARNS TO KNOW
JESUS CHRIST   *Frontispiece*
     F. Ross Maguire.

PATRICIUS TELLS HIS WIFE OF HIS DESIRE TO BE
A CHRISTIAN   53
     F. Ross Maguire.

ST. AUGUSTINE DECEIVES HIS MOTHER AND
SAILS AWAY TO ROME   90
     F. Ross Maguire.

"THE JOY OF THAT MOMENT WAS LIKE A FORE-
TASTE OF ETERNITY"   120
     From the picture by Ary Scheffer.

This book is above all things the story of a mother. But it is also the story of a noble woman—a woman who was truly great, for the reason that she never sought to be so. Because she understood the sphere in which a woman's work in the world must usually lie, and led her life truly along the lines that God had laid down for her ; because she suffered bravely, forgot herself for others, and remained faithful to her noble ideals, she ruled as a queen amongst those with whom her life was cast. Her influence was great and far-reaching, but she herself was the last to suspect it, the last to desire it, and that was perhaps the secret of its greatness. The type is rare at the present day, but, thank God! there are Monicas still in the world. If there were more, the world would be a better place.

CHAPTER I

HOW ST. MONICA WAS BROUGHT UP BY CHRISTIAN PARENTS IN THE CITY OF TAGASTE

ON the sunny northern coast of Africa in the country which we now call Algeria stood, in the early days of Christianity, a city called Tagaste. Not far distant lay the field of Zama, where the glory of Hannibal had perished for ever. But Rome had long since avenged the sufferings of her bitter struggle with Carthage. It was the ambition of Roman Africa, as the new colony had been called by its conquerors, to be, if possible, more Roman than Rome. Every town had its baths, its theatre, its circus, its temples, its aqueducts. It was forbidden even to exiles as a place of refuge—too much like home, said the authorities.

It was about the middle of the fourth century. The Church was coming forth from her long imprisonment into the light of day. The successor of Constantine, in name a Christian, sat on the Imperial throne. The old struggle with paganism, which had lasted for four hundred years, was nearly at an end, but new dangers assailed the Christian world. Men had found that it was easier to twist the truth than to deny it, and heresy and schism were abroad.

In the atrium or outer court of a villa on the outskirts of Tagaste an old woman and a young girl sat together looking out into the dark shadows of the evening, for the hot African sun had sunk not long since behind the Numidian Mountains, and the day had gone out like a lamp.

"And the holy Bishop Cyprian?" asked the girl.

"They sent him into exile," said the old woman, "for his father had been a Senator, and his family was well known and powerful. At that time they dared not put him to death, though later he, too, shed his blood for Christ. It was God's will that he should remain for many years to strengthen his flock in the trial."

"Did you ever see him, grandmother?" asked the girl.

"No," said the old woman, "it was before my time; but my mother knew him well. It was when he was a boy in Carthage and still a pagan that the holy martyrs Perpetua and Felicitas suffered with their companions. It was not till years after that he became a Christian, but it may have been their death that sowed the first seed in his heart."

"Tell me," said the girl softly. It was an oft-told tale of which she never tired. Her grandmother had lived through those dark days of persecution, and it was the delight of Monica's girlhood to hear her tell the stories of those who had borne witness to the Faith in their own land of Africa.

"Perpetua was not much older than you," said the old woman. "She was of noble race and born of a Christian mother, though her father was a pagan. She was married, and had a little infant of a few months' old. When she was called before the tribunal of Hilarion the Roman Governor, all were touched by her youth and beauty. 'Sacrifice to the gods,' they said, 'and you shall go

they might.

"Her old father hastened to he
the baby, and laid it in her arms.
leave your infant motherless?'
'and bring your old father's hair
to the grave?'

"'Have pity on the child!'
bystanders. 'Have pity on your

"Perpetua clasped her baby to
and her eyes filled with tears. Th
she had yielded, and brought her t

"'Just one little grain on the br
said, 'and you are free—for the
and your old father's.'

"She pushed it from her. 'I a
tian,' she said. 'God will keep m

"She was condemned with her
to be thrown to the wild beasts in
theatre, and they were taken awa
into a dark dungeon. Every day

1. One word, one little motion of
and they were free, restored again
appy life of old and the homes that
dear. There were many, alas! in
el days who had not courage for the
o sacrificed, and went their way.
ese weak women.

again they brought Perpetua her
d to try to shake her constancy.
on was like a palace,' she said, while
lowny head lay on her breast. Her
pt, and even struck her in his grief
. 'I am a Christian,' she said, and
back the babe.

were thrown to the wild beasts.
ind Perpetua, who had been tossed
cow, though horribly gored, were
. Gladiators were summoned to
1em. Felicitas died at the first
t the man's hand trembled, and he
Perpetua again and again, wounding

'Strike now,' she said, and so passed into the presence of her God."

Monica drew a long breath.

"So weak and yet so strong," she said.

"So it is, my child," said the old woman. "It is those who are strong and true in the little things of life who are strong and true in the great trials."

"It is hard to be always strong and true," said the girl.

"Not if God's love comes always first," answered the old woman.

Monica was silent. She was thinking of her own young life, and how, with all the safeguards of a Christian home about her, she had narrowly escaped a great danger. From her babyhood she had been brought up by her father's old nurse—not over-tenderly perhaps, but wisely, for the city of Tagaste was largely pagan in its habits, and the faithful old servant knew well what temptations would surround her nursling in later years. Monica, though full of life and spirit, had common sense and judgment beyond her years. She had also a great love of God and of all that belonged to His holy service, and would spend hours kneeling in the church in a quiet corner. It was there she brought all her childish troubles and her childish hopes; it was to the invisible Friend in the sanctuary that she confided all the secrets of her young heart, and, above all, that desire to suffer for Him and for His Church with which the stories of the martyrs had inspired her. When the time slipped away too fast, and she returned home late, she accepted humbly the correction that awaited her, for she knew that she had disobeyed—although **unintentionally**—her nurse's orders.

Monica had been wilfully disobedient once, and all her life long she would never forget the lesson her disobedience had taught her. It was a rule of her old nurse that she should take nothing to drink between meals, even in the hot days of summer in that sultry climate. If she had not courage to bear so slight a mortification as that, the old woman would argue, it would go ill with her in the greater trials of life. Monica had become used to the habit, but when she was old enough to begin to learn the duties of housekeeping her

day to the cellar to draw the wine for the midday meal. A maid-servant went with her to carry the flagon, and the child, feeling delightfully important, filled and refilled the little cup which was used to draw the wine from the cask and emptied it carefully into the wine-jar. When all was finished, a few drops remaining in the cup, a spirit of mischief took sudden possession of Monica, and she drained it off, making a wry face as she did so at the strange taste. The maid-servant laughed, and continued to laugh when the performance was repeated the next day and the day after. The strange taste became gradually less strange and less unpleasant to the young girl; daily a few drops were added, until at last, scarcely thinking what she did, she would drink nearly the fill of the little cup, while the servant laughed as of old.

But Monica was quick and intelligent, and was learning her household duties well. Finding one day that a piece of work which fell to the lot of the maid who went with her to the wine-cellar was very badly done, she reproved her severely. The woman turned on her young mistress angrily.

A LIFE'S LESSON

It is not for a wine-bibber like y
fault with me," she retorted.

onica stood horrified. The wo
lent word had torn the veil fror
. Whither was she drifting? Into
ths might that one act of disobedie1
tly committed have led her had no
[is mercy intervened? She never to
₂ for the rest of her life unless l;
ted with water. God had taugh
. " he who despises small things sha
ittle and little," and Monica had .
lesson. She had learnt to distrus1
and self-distrust makes one marvel
le with others; she had learnt, t(
her trust in God, and trust in God 1
marvellously strong. She had
;ht to love the poor and the suff
to serve them at her own expens(
nvenience, and the service of (
es one unselfish. God had worl
ica to do in His world, as He ha
ll if we will only do it, and He had

sat with her grandmother earlier in the day, she paused a moment and looked out between the tall pillars into the starlit night, where the palm-trees stood like dark shadows against the deep, deep blue of the sky. She clasped her hands, and her lips moved in prayer. "Oh God," she murmured, "to suffer for Thee and for Thy Faith!" God heard the whispered prayer, and answered it later. There is a living martyrdom as painful and as bitter as death, and Monica was called to taste it.

CHAPTER II

HOW ST. MONICA LIVED IN THE PAGAN HOUSEHOLD OF HER HUSBAND PATRICIUS

ALTHOUGH there were many Christians in Roman Africa, pagan manners and customs still survived in many of her cities. The people clung to their games in the circus, the cruel and bloody combats of the arena, which, though forbidden by Constantine, were still winked at by provincial governors They scarcely pretended to believe in their religion, but they held to the old pagan festivals, which enabled them to enjoy themselves without restraint under pretence of honouring the gods. The paganism of the fourth century, with its motto, " Let us eat, drink, and be merry," imposed no self-denial; it was therefore bound to be popular.

But unrestrained human nature is a dangerous thing. If men are content to live as the beasts that perish, they fall as far below their level as God meant them to rise above it, and the Roman Empire was falling to pieces through its own corruption. In Africa the worship of the old Punic gods, to whom living children used to be offered in sacrifice, had still its votaries, and priests of Saturn and Astarte, with their long hair and painted faces and scarlet robes, were still to be met dancing madly in procession through the streets of Carthage.

The various heretical sects had their preachers everywhere, proclaiming that there were much easier ways of serving Christ than that taught by the Catholic Church. It was hard for the Christian bishops to keep their flocks untainted, for there were enemies on every side.

When Monica was twenty-two years old her parents gave her in marriage to a citizen of Tagaste called Patricius. He held a good position in the town, for he belonged to a family which, though poor, was noble. Monica knew little of her future husband, save that he was nearly twice her age and a pagan, but it was the custom for parents to

rrange all such matters, and she had only
o obey.

A little surprise was perhaps felt in Tagaste
hat such good Christians should choose a
agan husband for their beautiful daughter,
ut it was found impossible to shake their
opeful views for the future. When it was
bjected that Patricius was well known for
is violent temper even amongst his own
ssociates, they answered that he would learn
entleness when he became a Christian. That
hings might go hard with their daughter in
he meantime they did not seem to foresee.

Monica took her new trouble where she
ad been used to take the old. Kneeling in
er favourite corner in the church, she asked
elp and counsel of the Friend Who never
ails. She had had her girlish ideals of love
nd marriage. She had dreamt of a strong
rm on which she could lean, of a heart and
oul that would be at one with her in all
hat was most dear, of two lives spent to-
ether in God's love and service. And now

into the light of truth. Would she succeed? And if not, what would be that married life which lay before her? She did not dare to think. She must not fail—and yet. . . . " Thou in me, O Lord," she prayed again and again through her tears.

It was late when she made her way homewards, and that night, kneeling at her bedside, she laid the ideals of her girlhood at the feet of Him Who lets no sacrifice, however small, go unrewarded. She would be true to this new trust, she resolved, cost what it might.

Things certainly did not promise well for the young bride's happiness. Patricius lived with his mother, a woman of strong passions like himself, and devoted to her son. She was bitterly jealous of the young girl who had stolen his affections, and had made up her mind to dislike her. The slaves of the household followed, of course, their mistress's lead, and tried to please her by inventing stories against Monica.

Patricius, who loved his young wife with the only kind of love of which he was capable, had nothing in common with her, and had no clue to her thoughts or actions. He had neither reverence nor respect for women—indeed, most of the women of his acquaintance were deserving of neither—and he had chosen Monica for her beauty, much as he would have chosen a horse or a dog. He thought her ways and ideas extraordinary. She took as kindly an interest in the slaves as if they had been of her own flesh and blood, and would even intercede to spare them a beating. She liked the poor, and would gather these dirty and unpleasant people about her, going so far even as to wash and dress their sores. Patricius did not share her attraction, and objected strongly to such proceedings; but Monica pleaded so humbly and sweetly that he gave way, and let her do what seemed to cause her so much pleasure. "There was no accounting for tastes," he remarked. She would spend hours in the church praying, with her great eyes fixed on the altar. True, she was never there at any time when she was likely to be missed by her husband, and never was she so full of tender affection for him as when she came home; but still, it was a strange way of

is something about Monica, it is
was altogether unlike any other
he house, as she went about her
, always watching for the chance
kind action.
tricius was in one of his violent
outing, abusing, and even striking
who came in his way, she would
n with gentle eyes that showed
 nor anger. She never answered
n though his rude words wounded
. He had once raised his hand
er, but he had not dared; some-
 did not know what — withheld

hen his anger had subsided, and
aps a little ashamed of his violence,
 meet him with an affectionate
ving and forgetting all. Only if
mself, and, touched at her gene-
rance, tried shamefacedly to make

preached not at all, loved much, and prayed unceasingly."

When the young wives of her acquaintance, married like herself to pagan husbands, complained of the insults and even blows which they had to bear, " Are you sure your own tongue is not to blame?" she would ask them laughingly; and then with ready sympathy would do all she could to help and comfort and advise. They would ask her secret, for everyone knew that, in spite of the violence of Patricius's temper, he treated her with something that almost approached respect. Then she would bid them be patient, and love and pray, and meet harshness with gentleness, and abuse with silence. And when

To the outside world **Patricius's** young wife seemed contented and happy. She managed her affairs well, people said, and no one but God knew of the suffering that was her secret and His. Brought up in the peace and piety of a Christian family, she had had no idea of the miseries of paganism. Now she had ample opportunity to study the effects of unchecked selfishness and of uncontrolled passions; to see how low human nature, unrestrained by faith and love, could fall. Her mother-in-law treated her with suspicion and dislike, for the slaves, never weary of inventing fresh stories against her, misrepresented all her actions to their mistress. Monica did not seem to notice unkindness, repaying the many insults she received with little services tactfully rendered, but she felt it deeply.

"They do not know," she would say to herself, and pray for them all the more earnestly, offering her sufferings for these poor souls who were so far from the peace of

if not through her? How could they learn to love Christ unless they learned to love His

revelation must come through her, if it was to come at all. "Thou in me, O Lord," she would pray, and draw strength and courage at His feet for the daily suffering.

The heart of Patricius was like a neglected garden. Germs of generosity, of nobility, lay hidden under a rank growth of weeds that no one had ever been at any trouble to clear away. The habits of a lifetime held him captive. With Monica he was always at his best, but he grew weary of being at his best. It was so much easier to be at his worst. He gradually began to seek distractions amongst his old pagan companions in the old ignoble pleasures.

The whole town began to talk of his neglect of his beautiful young wife. Monica suffered cruelly, but in silence. When he was at home, which was but seldom, she was serene and gentle as usual. She never reproached him, and treated him with the same tender deference as of old. Patricius felt the charm of her presence; all that was good in him responded; but evil habits had gone far to stifle the good, and his lower nature cried out for base enjoyments He was not

Monica wept and prayed in secret, and sent a ray of sunshine to brighten her life. Three children were born to her ng the early years of her marriage. The e of Augustine, her eldest son, will be ver associated with that of his mother. he other two, **Navigius** and Perpetua his r, we know little. **Navigius**, delicate in h, was of **a** gentle and pious nature. he and Perpetua married, but the latter her husband's death entered a monas-

With her younger children Monica no trouble; it was the eldest, Augustine, after having been for long the son of sorrow and of her prayers, was destined **at** last her glory and her joy.

CHAPTER III

HOW ST. MONICA BROUGHT UP HER CHIL[D]
AND HOW THE LITTLE AUGUSTINE [FELL]
SICK AND DESIRED BAPTISM

As soon as the little Augustine was bor[n his]
[m]other had him taken to the Chr[istian]
[C]hurch, that the sign of the Cross mig[ht be]
[m]ade on his forehead, and that he mig[ht be]
[e]ntered amongst the catechumens. It [was the]
[c]ustom of the time—never approved of [by the]
[C]hurch—to put off Baptism until the cat[echu]-
[me]nen had shown himself able to with[stand]
[t]he temptations of the half-pagan socie[ty in]
[t]he midst of which he had to live. Th[is]

The outlook for Monica, with her pagan husband and her pagan household, was darker than for most Christian mothers. Her heart grew heavy within her as she held her young son in her arms and thought of the future. For the present indeed he was hers; but later, when she could no longer keep him at her side and surround him with a mother's love and protection, what dangers would beset him? The influence of an unbelieving father, during the years when his boyish ideas of life would be forming; a household that knew not Christ—how could he pass untouched through the dangers that would assail his young soul? With prayers and tears, Monica bent over the unconscious little head that lay so peacefully upon her breast, commending her babe to the Heavenly Father to Whom all things are possible.

Augustine drank in the love of Christ with his mother's milk, he tells us. As soon as he could speak, she taught him to lisp a prayer. As soon as he could understand, she taught him, in language suited to his childish sense, the great truths of the Christian Faith. He would listen eagerly, and, standing at his mother's knee, or nestling in her arms, follow the sweet voice that could make the highest things so simple to his childish understanding.

It was the seed-time that was later to bear such glorious fruit, though the long days of winter lay between. The boy was thoughtful and intelligent; he loved all that was great and good and noble. The loathing of what was mean and base and unlovely, breathed into him by his mother in those days of early childhood, haunted him even during his worst moments in later life. The cry that burst from his soul in manhood when he had drunk deeply of the cup of earthly joys and found it bitter and unsatisfying had its origin in those early teachings. "Thou hast made us for Thyself, O God, and our hearts can find no rest until they rest in Thee."

One day, when the child was about seven years old, he was suddenly seized with sickness. He was in great pain, and soon became so ill that his life was in danger. His parents were in anguish, but Augustine's

Monica added her entreaties to his. Patricius yielded. All was prepared, when the child suddenly got better. Then someone intervened, probably his father, for Augustine tells us that the Baptism was put off again—indefinitely.

But it was time to think of the boy's education, and it was proposed to send him to school in Tagaste. It was a pagan school to which the child must go, pagan authors that he must study, and, worse than all, pagan conversation that he must hear and pagan playmates with whom he must associate.

Patricius was proud of the beauty and the intelligence of his little son, and hoped great things for the future; but Augustine's early school-days were far from brilliant. Eager as the boy was to learn what interested him, he had an insurmountable dislike to anything that caused him trouble. It bored him to learn to read and write, and the uninspiring truth that two and two make four was a weariness of the flesh to him. Though the stories of Virgil enchanted him, Homer he never thoroughly enjoyed nor quite forgave, for had he not for his sake been forced to wade through the chilly waters of the Greek grammar?

Unfortunately for Augustine, such dismal truths as two and two make four have to be mastered before higher flights can be attempted. The Tagaste schoolmasters had but one way of sharpening their scholars' zeal for learning — the liberal use of the rod.

Now, Augustine disliked beatings as much as he disliked all other unpleasant things, but he also disliked work. The only way of evading both disagreeables was to follow the example of the greater number of his fellow-scholars—to play when he should have been working, and to tell clever lies to his schoolmasters and his parents in order to escape punishment. Such tricks, however, are bound to be found out sooner or later, and Monica, realizing that much could be got out of her son by love, but little by fear, took him for a course of instruction to the Christian priests, that he might learn to overcome himself for the love of God.

As a result Augustine took more earnestly

to his prayers, asking, above all, however, that he might not be beaten at school. His mother, finding him one day praying in a quiet corner to this intent, suggested that if he had learnt his lessons for the day he need have no fear, but if he had not, punishment was to be expected. Patricius, who was passing and overheard the conversation, laughed at his son's fears and agreed with his wife. Augustine thought them both exceedingly heartless.

As the boy grew older, however, his wonderful gifts began to show themselves, and his masters, seeing of what he was really capable, punished him yet more severely when he was idle. Augustine, too, began to take pride in his own success, and to wish to be first amongst his young companions. The latter cheated as a matter of course, both in work and at play. Bad habits are catching, and Augustine would sometimes cheat too. When found out he would fly into a passion, although no one was so severe on the dishonesty of others as he. And yet, though he would often yield to the temptations that were the hardest for his pleasure-loving nature to resist, there was much that was good in the boy. He had a faithful and loving heart, an attraction for all that was great and noble. He was, in fact, his mother's son as well as his father's; the tares and the wheat were sprouting side by side.

But Augustine was rapidly growing out of childhood. Patricius, prouder than ever of his clever son, resolved to spare no pains to give him the best education that his means could procure. The boy had a great gift of eloquence, said his masters, and much judgment; he would be certain to succeed brilliantly at the Bar. It was decided to send him to Madaura, a town about twenty miles distant, a good deal larger than Tagaste, and well known for its culture and its schools. It was one of the most pagan of the cities of Africa, but this was an objection that had no weight with Patricius, although it meant much to Monica. The only comfort for her in the thought of this first separation was that there at least her son would not be far from home. Not far away in truth, as distance goes, but how far away in spirit!

Madaura was a large and handsome city, with a circus and theatre, and a fine forum,

ket-place, set round with statues of
 ls. It was proud of its reputation
 ning, but had little else to be proud of.
)fessors were men who were more
 d of being detected in a fault of style
 the grossest crimes, who were ashamed
 of nothing else. The pagan gods were
 p to their scholars as models for
 :ion and imitation.
 is a poor ideal at the best. The gods
 :presented by the great pagan poets
 thors as no better, if more powerful,
 :dinary mortals. They were subject
 :he meannesses and all the baseness
 east noble of their worshippers. That
 .dventures, neither moral nor ele-
 were told in the most exquisite lan-
)y the greatest authors of antiquity
 added to the danger than decreased
 ιe, the noblest of the classical writers

masters. Nothing was too shameful t(
lked about, if only it were talked abou
ell-turned phrases. The plays acted in
heatre were what might be expected in
an society of the fourth century—tha
y from which St. Anthony and St
ne had been forced to flee to the deser
der to save their souls.

gustine won golden opinions from hi
ers for his quickness and intelligence
thought of nothing else but of culti
g the minds of their scholars. Hear
soul were left untouched, or touched in
a way that evil sprang to life and goo(
stifled. He was a genius, they cried, a
ing rhetorician, a poet.

though masters and scholars alike ap
led him, Augustine, while he drank thei
es greedily, was restless and unhappy
ad gone down before the subtle tempta
of Madaura like corn before the scythe
evil thoughts, but carelessly resisted

CHAPTER IV

HOW ST. MONICA BY HER GENTLENESS AN[D] CHARITY WON PATRICIUS AND HIS MOTHE[R] TO CHRIST

OF all the hidden forces in the world perhap[s] the most mysterious is what we call "i[n]fluence." For good or for evil, to a lesser [or] a greater degree, it goes out from each o[ne] of us, and has its effect on all with whom w[e]

downward push to all who come in contact with us. Happily for us all, God does not ask of us attainment, but effort, and earnest effort is the simple secret of healthy influence.

Monica, it is true, was a Saint, but a Saint in the making. Saints are not born ready-made; holiness is a beautiful thing that is built up stone by stone, not brought into being by the touch of the enchanter's wand.

During the years that had passed since Patricius had brought his young wife home to his mother's house, she would have been the first to confess how far she had fallen short of the ideal she had set herself to attain. And yet there had been ceaseless effort, ceaseless prayer, unwearying love and patience. Outwardly all seemed as usual, but the hidden force had been doing its work in secret—as it always does.

The mother of Patricius was growing old; she was neither so active nor so strong as she had been. What had used to be easy to her was becoming difficult. It galled her independent spirit to be obliged to ask help of others. Monica, reading her heart as only **the unselfish** can, saw this **and** understood.

At every moment the older woman wo
ind that some little service had been d
y unseen hands, some little thoughtful
hat made things easier for the tired
imbs. There was someone who seemed
now and understand what she wan
lmost before she did herself.

Who could it be? Not the slaves, c
ainly. They did their duty for fear of be
eaten, but that was all. It was all, inde
hat was expected of them. Not Patrie
ither; it was not his way, he never thoug
f such things. It could therefore be no
ut Monica.

The old woman mused deeply. She h
reated her daughter-in-law harshly and
indly during all these years. She h
ooked upon her as an intruder. But th

unkindness? With never-failing charity and sweetness, with gentle respect and deference to her wishes, never trying to assert herself, never appealing to her husband to give her the place which of right belonged to her. She had been content to be treated as the last in the house.

The old woman sat lost in thought. What would the house be like, she suddenly asked herself, without that gentle presence? What would she do, what would they all do, without Monica? With a sudden pang of sorrow she realized how much she leant upon her daughter-in-law, what her life would be without her. She considered the matter in this new light. She was a woman of strong passions but of sound common sense; reason was beginning to triumph over prejudice.

Sending for the slaves, she questioned them sharply as to the tales they had told her about their young mistress. They faltered, contradicted each other and themselves—in the end confessed that they had lied.

The old lady went straight to her son, and told him the whole story. Patricius was not one to take half measures in such a matter.

Not even the prayers of Monica, all unconscious of the particular offence they had committed, availed to save the culprits. They were as soundly beaten as they had ever been in their lives, after which they were told that they knew what to expect if they ever breathed another word against their young mistress again. As it happened, they had no desire to do so. The hidden forces had been working there too. Monica's kindness, her sympathy with their joys and sorrows—to them something strange and new—had already touched their hearts. More than once they had been sorry for ever having spoken against her; they had felt ashamed in her presence.

Justice having been done on the slaves, the mother of Patricius sought out her daughter-in-law, told her frankly that she had been in the wrong, and asked her forgiveness. Monica clasped the old woman in her arms and refused to listen. From that moment they were the truest of friends.

There were many things to be spoken of, but first religion. Monica had revealed her Faith by her life, her daily actions, and to the other it was a beautiful and alluring revelation. She wanted to know, to understand; she listened eagerly to Monica's explanations.

It was a message of new life, of hope beyond the grave, of joy, of peace; she begged to be received as a catechumen. It was not long before she knelt at Monica's side before the altar to be signed on the brow with the Cross of Christ—the joyous first-fruits of the seed that had been sown in tears.

One by one the slaves followed their mistress's example, hungering in their turn for the message that brought such peace and light to suffering and weary souls. Was it for such as they? they asked. And Monica answered that it was for all, that the Master Himself had chosen to be as One that served.

The whole household was Christian now, with the exception of Patricius, and even he was growing daily more gentle, more thoughtful; the mysterious forces were working on him too. His love for Monica was more reverent; his eyes were opening slowly to the beauty of spiritual things. The old life,

its old pleasures, was growing distasteful
[h]im; he saw its baseness while as yet he
[coul]d scarcely tear himself free from its
[fett]ers—the fetters of old habit so hard to
[brea]k. He noticed the change in his mother,
[and] half-envied her her courage. He even
[envi]ed the slaves their happy faces, the new
[ligh]t that shone in their eyes and that gave
[the]m a strange new dignity.

[M]onica, watching the struggle, redoubled
[her] prayers; her unselfish love surrounded
[her] husband like an atmosphere of light and
[swe]etness, drawing him with an invincible
[pow]er to better things. She would speak to
[him] of their children—above all, of Augustine,
[thei]r eldest-born, the admiration of his
[mas]ters at Madaura. He was astonishing
[eve]rybody, they wrote, by his brilliant gifts.
[He] had the soul of a poet and the eloquence
[of a]n orator; he would do great things.

[M]adaura had been all very well up till now,
[the] father decided, but everything must be
[don]e to give their boy a good start in life;
[the]y must go farther afield. Rome was

were limited, but he resolved to do his utmost for his eldest son. Carthage had a reputation for culture and for learning that was second only to that of Rome. If strict economy were practised at home, Carthage might be possible. In the meantime it was not much use leaving the boy at Madaura. Let him come home and remain there a year, during which he could study privately while they saved the money to pay his expenses at Carthage.

The suggestion delighted Monica. She would have her son with her for a whole year. She would be able to watch over him just when he needed her motherly care; she looked forward eagerly to Augustine's return. The old, intimate life they had led together before he went to Madaura would begin again. Again her boy would hang on her arm and tell her all his hopes and dreams for the future—hopes and dreams into which she always entered, of which she was always part. She would look once more into the boy's clear eyes while he confessed to her his faults and failings, and see the light flame up in them as she told him of noble and heroic deeds, and urged him to be true to his ideals.

And so in happy dreams the days went past until Augustine's return; but there was bitter grief in store for Monica. This was not the same Augustine that they had left at Madaura two years ago. The days of the old familiar friendship seemed to have gone past recall. His eyes no longer turned to her with the old candour; he shunned her questioning look. He shunned her company even, and seemed more at ease with his father, who was proud beyond words of his tall, handsome son.

He was all right, said Patricius; he was growing up, that was all. Boys could not always be tied to their mother's apron-strings. The moment that Monica had so dreaded for Augustine had come then; the pagan influences had been at work. Oh, she did not enter, other thoughts far away—how far away!—from hers. A dark cloud was between them.

One day she persuaded her son to go out with her. The spring had just come—that wonderful African spring when the whole world seems suddenly to burst into flower. Asphodels stood knee-deep on either side of the path in which they walked; the fragrance of the springtime was in their nostrils; the golden sunlight bathed the rainbow earth. It was a walk that they had loved to take of old, to delight together in all the beauty of that world which God had made.

Monica spoke gently to her son of the new life that lay before him, of the dangers that beset his path. He must hold fast to the Law of Christ, she told him; he must be pure and strong and true.

There was no answering gleam as of old. The boy listened with a bad grace—shame and honour were tugging at his heart-strings, but in vain. The better self was defeated, for

PATRICIUS TELLS HIS WIFE OF HIS DESIRE TO BE A CHRISTIAN.

speak to her, he said. She slipped her arm into his, smiling through her pain, and they went back again, between the nodding asphodels and the hedges of wisteria, along the path she had just trodden with her son.

There was an unwonted seriousness about Patricius. He had been thinking deeply of late, he told her. He had begun to see things in a new light. It was dim as yet, and he was still weak; but the old life and the old religion had grown hateful to him. Her God was the true God; he wanted to know how to love and serve that God of hers. Was he fit, did she think, to learn? Could he be received as a catechumen?

The new joy fell like balm on the new sorrow. Monica had lost her son, but gained her husband. God was good. He had heard her prayers, He had accepted her sacrifice. Surely He would give her back her boy. She would trust on and hope. " He will withhold

heart? Was it the last struggle be[tween] good and evil? Was the influence [of his] mother, the love of Christ she had in[stilled] into him in his childhood, making o[ne last] stand against the influences that had s[wayed] him in Madaura—that still swayed hin[, the] influences of the corrupt world in wh[ich he] lived? We do not know. If it was s[o, the] evil triumphed.

CHAPTER V

AUGUSTINE WENT TO CARTHAGE, AND PATRICIUS DIED A CHRISTIAN DEATH

[T]INE's year at home did not do for [wh]at Monica had hoped. His old pagan [fe]llows gathered round him; he was [ ] with them; the happy home-life [   ] to have lost its charm. The want [of prin]ciple and of honour in most of them [shock]ed him in his better moments; never[theless] he was content to enjoy himself in [their co]mpany. He was even ashamed, when [they bo]asted of their misdoings, to seem more [innocen]t than they, and would pretend to be [worse t]han he really was, lest his prestige [should] suffer in their eyes. There were [momen]ts when he loathed it all, and longed [for the] old life, with its innocent pleasures; [but it i]s hard to turn back on the downhill

ot care to eat them, and threw them to
pigs. It was not schoolboy greed that
pted the theft, but the pure delight of
 evil, of tricking the owner of the garden.
e was the wild excitement, too, of the
g; the fear that they might be caught
e act. He was careful to keep such
ades a secret from his mother; but
ca was uneasy, knowing what might be
cted from the companions her son had
en.
tricius was altogether unable to give
stine the help that he needed. The
tian ideals of life and conduct were new
im as yet; the old pagan ways seemed
 natural. He was scarcely likely to be
ished at the fact that his son's boyhood
rather like what his own had been. He
tanding, it is true, on the threshold of the
ch, but her teaching was not yet clear to
 His own feet were not firm enough in

the ways of Christ to enable him to stretch a steadying hand to another.

His mother was failing fast; the end could not be far off. Monica was devoting herself heart and soul to the old woman, who clung to her with tender affection, and was never happy in her absence.

Patricius watched them together, and marvelled at the effects of the grace of Baptism. Was that indeed his mother, he asked himself, that gentle, patient old woman, so thoughtful for others, so ready to give up her own will? She had used to be violent and headstrong like himself, resentful and implacable in her dislikes, but now she was more like Monica than like him. That was Monica's way, though; her sweetness and patience seemed to be catching. She was like the sunshine, penetrating everywhere with its light and warmth. He, alas! was far behind his mother. Catechumen though he was, the old temper would often flash out still. Self-conquest was the hardest task that he had ever undertaken, and sometimes he almost lost heart, and was inclined to give it up altogether. Then Monica would gently remind him that with God's help the hardest things were possible, and they would kneel and pray together, and Patricius would take heart again for the fight. She had a wonderful gift for giving people courage; Patricius had noticed that before. He supposed it was because she was so full of sympathy, and always made allowances. And then she seemed to think—to be sure, even—that if one went on trying, failures did not matter, God did not mind them; and that was a very comforting reflection for poor weak people like himself. To go on trying was possible even for him, although he knew he could not always promise himself success.

Patricius was anxious about Augustine's future. All his efforts had not succeeded in saving the sum required for his first year at Carthage. He had discovered that it would cost a good deal more than he had at first supposed, and it was difficult to see where the money was to come from.

It was at this moment that Romanianus, a wealthy and honourable citizen of Tagaste, who knew the poverty of his friend, came for-

The old boyish laziness had give
real zeal for learning and thirst aft
;e. The idle life at home was ce
e worst thing for him. Hard wor
pursuit of wisdom might steady h
ure and bring him back to God.
only hope now, as with prayers an
e besought of Him to watch ov

onica did not know Carthage. If
nd only to Rome for its culture an
ls, it almost rivalled Rome in i
n. There all that was worst in tl
n of the East and of the West m
gled. The bloody combats betwee
beasts, the gladiatorial shows th:
the Romans, were free to а

Carthage. Such plays as the Romans delighted in, impossible to describe, were acted in the theatre. The horrible rites of the Eastern religions were practised openly.

There was neither discipline nor order in the schools. The wealthier students gloried in their bad reputation. They were young men of fashion who were capable of anything, and who were careful to let others know it. They went by the name of "smashers" or "upsetters," from their habit of raiding the schools of professors whose teaching they did not approve, and breaking everything on which they could lay hands. They treated new-comers with coarse brutality, but Augustine seems in some manner to have escaped their enmity. Perhaps a certain dignity in the young man's bearing, or perhaps his brilliant gifts, won their respect, for he surpassed them all in intelligence, and speedily outstripped them in class.

Augustine was eager for knowledge and eager for enjoyment. He frequented the theatre; his pleasure-loving nature snatched at everything that life could give; yet he was not happy. "My God," he cried in

ANSWERED PRAYERS 61

later years, "with what bitter gall didst Thou in Thy great mercy sprinkle those pleasures of mine!" He could not forget; and at Tagaste his mother was weeping and praying for her son.

Patricius prayed with her; he understood at last. Every day the germs of a noble nature that had lain so long dormant within him were gaining strength and life. Every day his soul was opening more and more to the understanding of spiritual things, while Monica watched the transformation with a heart that overflowed with gratitude and love. The sorrows of the past were all forgotten in the joy of the present, that happy union at the feet of Christ. There was but one cause for sadness—Patricius's health was failing. His mother had already shown him the joys of a Christian deathbed. She had passed away smiling, with their hands in hers, and the name of Jesus on her lips. The beautiful prayers of the Church had gone down with the departing soul to the threshold of the new life, and had followed it into eternity. She seemed close to them still in the light of that wonderful new Faith, and to be waiting for them in their everlasting home.

But Monica's happiness was to be short-lived, for it seemed that Patricius would soon rejoin his mother. He did not deceive himself. He spoke of his approaching death to Monica, and asked her to help him to make a worthy preparation for Baptism, which he desired to receive as soon as possible. With the simplicity and trustfulness of a child, he looked to her for guidance, and did all that she desired.

The ceremony over, he turned to his wife and smiled. A wonderful peace possessed him. The old life, with all its stains, had passed from him in those cleansing waters; the new life was at hand. Once more he asked her to forgive him all the pain he had caused her, all that he had made her suffer. No, she must not grieve, he told her; the parting would be but for a little while, the meeting for all eternity. She had been his angel, he said; he owed all his joy to her. It was her love, her patience, that had done it all. She had shown him the beauty of goodness and made him love it. He thanked her

CHAPTER VI

HOW ST. MONICA LIVED IN THE DAYS OF HER WIDOWHOOD, AND HOW SHE PUT ALL HER TRUST IN GOD

PATRICIUS had not much in the way of worldly goods to leave to his wife. She needed little, it is true, for herself, but there was Augustine. Would it be possible for her, even if she practised the strictest economy, to keep him at Carthage, where he was doing so well?

Romanianus divined her anxiety, and hastened to set it at rest. He had a house in Carthage, he said; it should be Augustine's as long as he required it. This would settle the question of lodging. For the rest, continued Romanianus, as an old friend of Patricius he had the right to befriend his son, and Monica must grant him the privilege of acting a father's part to Augustine until

Monica would befriend his boy, they would be quits. The gratitude of both mother and son towards this generous friend and benefactor lasted throughout their lives. Licentius was to feel its effects more than once.

"You it was, Romanianus," wrote Augustine in his *Confessions*, "who, when I was a poor young student in Carthage, opened to me your house, your purse, and still more your heart. You it was who, when I had the sorrow to lose my father, comforted me by your friendship, helped me with your advice, and assisted me with your fortune."

Monica mourned her husband's death with true devotion; but hers was not a selfish sorrow. She had love and sympathy for all who needed them, and forgot her own grief in solacing that of others. There were certain good works which the Church gave to Christian widows to perform. The hospitals, for instance, were entirely in their hands.

These devoted women succeeded each other at intervals in their task of washing and attending to the sick, watching by their beds and cleaning their rooms. Their ministrations did not even cease there. With reverent care they prepared the dead for burial, thinking the while of the preparation of Christ's body for the tomb, and of Him who said: " Inasmuch as ye do it to the least of My brethren ye do it unto Me."

It was a happy moment for Monica when her turn came to serve the sick. She would kiss their sores for very pity as she washed and dressed them, and their faces grew bright at her coming. They called her " mother." It seemed such a natural name to give her, for she was a mother to them all, and gave them a mother's love. To some of the poor creatures, friendless slaves as they often were, who had known little sympathy or tenderness in their hard lives, it was a revelation of Christianity which taught them more than hours of preaching could have done.

But there was other work besides that at the hospital. There were the poor to be helped, the hungry to be fed, the naked

ry poor, she would keep them in
/n house, feed them at her own table,
)the them with her own hands. "If]
 mother to these motherless ones,"
)uld say to herself, "He will have m
ιd give me back my boy; if I teach t
 know and love Him as a Father, He
ιtch over my son."

It was a custom of the time on the fe
 saints and martyrs to make a pilgrin
 their tombs, with a little basket of .
ιd wine. This was laid on the grave, ε
ιich the faithful would partake of v
ey had brought, while they thought
oke of the noble lives of God's serv
10 had gone before. The custom
olished not long after on account of
ιuses which had arisen, but Monica obse
 to the end. She scarcely tasted of
!ering herself, but gave it all away to
or. Often, indeed, she went cold
ιngry that they might be clothed and .

scope. Every morning found her in her place in church for the Holy Sacrifice; every evening she was there again, silent, absorbed in God. The place where she knelt was often wet with her tears; the time passed by unheeded. Patricius, her husband, was safe in God's hands; but Augustine, her eldest-born, her darling, in what dark paths was he wandering? And yet in her heart of hearts there was a deep conviction that no sad news of his life at Carthage could shake. His was not the nature to find contentment in the things of earth. He was born to something higher. His noble heart, his strong intelligence, would bring him back to God.

And yet, and yet . . . her heart sank as she thought of graces wasted, of conscience trampled underfoot, of light rejected. No, there was no hope anywhere but with God. In Him she would trust, and in Him alone. He was infinite in mercy, and strong to save. He had promised that He would never fail those who put their trust in Him. At His feet, and at His feet alone, Monica poured out her tears and her sorrow. With others she was serene and hopeful as of old, even joyous, always ready to help and comfort. It was said of her after her death that no one had such a gift of helping others as she. She never preached at people—most people have an insurmountable dislike to being preached at—but every word she said had a strange power of drawing souls to God, of making them wish to be better.

Augustine, meanwhile, at Carthage, was justifying all the hopes that had been formed of him. He had even greater gifts, it seemed, than eloquence, feeling, and wit. He was at the head of his class in rhetoric. His master had spoken to him of a certain treatise of Aristotle which he would soon be called upon to study. It was so profound, he said, that few could understand it, even with the help of the most learned professors. Augustine, eager to make acquaintance with this wonderful work, procured it at once and read it. It seemed to him perfectly simple; it was unnecessary, he found, to ask a single explanation.

It was the same with geometry, music, every science he took up. This young genius of nineteen only discovered there were diffi-

culties in the way when he
others, and realized how hard
them understand what was
simple to himself.

There was something strang
and attractive about Augusti
modest and reserved about
although he himself tells us in
that he was full of pride and
had a gift of making true and
a charm in conversation that
companions and even older n

A more worldly mother tha
have been thoroughly prou
Faith and virtue were alone
in that soul that could so ill d

already he felt the emptiness of earthly joys. " I longed, my God," he writes, " to fly from the things of earth to Thee, and I knew not that it was Thou that wast working in me. . . ."

" One thing cooled my ardour," he goes on to say; " it was that the Name of Christ was not there, and this Name, by Thy mercy, Lord, of Thy Son, my Saviour, my heart had drawn in with my mother's milk, and kept in its depths, and every doctrine where this Name did not appear, fluent, elegant, and truth-like though it might be, could not master me altogether."

He then turned to the Holy Scriptures, but they appeared to him inferior in style to Cicero. " My pride," he writes, " despised the manner in which the things are said, and my intelligence could not discover the hidden sense. They become great only for the humble, and I disdained to humble myself, and, inflated with vainglory, I believed myself great."

It was at this moment that he came in contact with the Manicheans, whose errors attracted him at once. This extraordinary

ns they used Christian words for
that were thoroughly unchrist
 the most remarkable thing ab
is their hatred of the Church. Au
to remained amongst them for
hus describes them when writing
:
u knowest, Honoratus, that for
alone did we fall into the hands
en—namely, that they professed
from all errors, and bring us to
reason alone, without that terr
of authority. For what else
le to abandon the faith of my ch
d follow these men for almost
ut their assertion that we were to
superstition into a faith blindly
pon our reason, while they urged
elieve until the truth was fully
and proved? Who would not

That was what the Manicheans promised, [and] that Augustine found amongst them he also tells us.

"They incessantly repeated to me, 'Truth, Truth,' but there was no truth in them; they taught what was false, not only about Thee, my God, Who art the very Truth, but even about the elements of this world, Thy creatures."

So much for their doctrines; as for the teachers themselves, he found them "carnal and loquacious, full of insane pride."

The great charm of Manicheism to Augustine was that it taught that a man was not responsible for his sins. This doctrine was convenient to one who could not find the strength to break with his bad habits.

"Such was my mind," he sums up later, looking back on this period of his life, "so weighed down, so blinded by the flesh, that I was myself unknown to myself."

carcely joined the Manicheans bef
idings reached **Monica**. At first sh
ardly believe it. This was a blow fo
he had not been prepared; it crushec
he earth. She would have grieved l
he news of her son's death.

And yet she bent her broken heart t
ill, and hoped on in Him " Whose
annot fail." Augustine had renoun
aith of his childhood publicly, she
iter; he had been entered by the Man
s an " auditor," the first degree of in
i their sect. And with all the ze
rdour that he carried into everything
e was advocating this abominable

and persuading his companions to follow his example.

Her eyes grew dim with weeping for her son. He was dead indeed to God—that God who was her All in All. The vacation was near, and Augustine would then return to Tagaste. Perhaps she would find that it was not so bad as she had thought. It might be only the whim of a moment; she would wait and see.

Alas! the hope was vain. Augustine had scarcely been a day at home before he began obstinately to air his new opinions, determined that she should listen. Then the Christian in Monica rose above the mother; her horror of heresy was for the moment stronger than her love for her son. Standing before him, outraged and indignant, she told him plainly that if he spoke in such a way she could no longer receive him at her table or in her house.

Augustine was amazed; he had found out at last the limits of his mother's endurance. With bent head he left the house and sought the hospitality of Romanianus. No sooner had he gone than Monica's heart melted, the

...m which brought her a strange s...
...e and comfort.

...seemed to her that she was stand...
...arrow rule or plank of wood, he...
...ghed down with sorrow as it ha...
...through the day. Suddenly there...
...ards her a young man radiant a...
...ace. Smiling at her, he asked th...
...er tears. "I am weeping," she an...
...r the loss of my son." "Grieve n...
...," he replied, "for, look, your...
...ding there beside you." Monica...
...head. It was true; Augustine s...
...side on the plank of wood. "Be...
...r," continued the stranger, "for...
...are there shall he be also." Then...
...ke; the words were ringing in he...
...emed to her that God had spoken.
...the morning she went straight to...
...and told him of her dream. "Pe...
...ested her son, anxious to turn it...

own advantage, "it means that you will come to see things as I do." "No," said Monica firmly, "for he did not say, 'Where *he* is *you* shall be,' but, 'Where *you* are there *he* shall be.'" Augustine was even more struck by the earnestness of his mother's answer than by the dream itself, though he pretended to make light of both.

Not long after Monica went to see a certain holy Bishop, that she might beg him to use his influence with Augustine to bring him back to the truth. The wise old man listened attentively to her story. "Let him alone for the present, but pray much," was his advice, "for as yet he is obstinate and puffed up with these new ideas. If what you tell me of your son is true, he will read for himself, and will find out his error." Then, seeing the anguish of the poor mother, he told her that he himself in his youth had been led away by the Manicheans, and had even been employed in transcribing their works. It was that which had saved him; for, as he wrote, the truth became clear to him; he had seen how much their doctrines were to be avoided. Then, as Monica wept for disappointment—for she had counted greatly on his help—a sudden pity seized him. "Go thy ways, and God bless thee," he cried. "It is impossible that a son of such tears should perish."

Monica's dream and the words of the Bishop were like rays of light in the darkness. She drew fresh hope from them and redoubled her prayers.

The vacation drew to an end, and Augustine returned to Carthage, but not for long. He was now twenty years old. His friend and patron, Romanianus, was very anxious that he should open a school in Tagaste while waiting for something better, and this he resolved to do. A little circle of pupils soon gathered round him, who were later to follow their young master in all his wanderings. Amongst these was Alypius, an old schoolfellow and a devoted friend; the sons of Romanianus; and another friend of Augustine's childhood whose name we do not know, but who was dearer to him than all the rest. They were of the same age, had studied together, had the same tastes, and the same ambitions.

Influenced by Augustine, still warm in the

praise of the Manicheans, he, as well as the rest, had abjured the Catholic faith to join their heresy.

Augustine had been about a year at Tagaste when this friend was taken suddenly ill. He lay unconscious in a burning fever; there seemed to be no hope of recovery. He had been a catechumen before he had joined the Manicheans. His parents, who were Christians, having begged that he might be baptized before he died, the life-giving waters were poured on him as he lay between life and death. Augustine made no protest, so sure was he that what he himself had taught him before he was taken ill would have more influence than a rite administered without his knowledge or consent. To everybody's surprise the young man recovered his senses and began to mend.

Augustine then laughingly told him what they had been doing, and went on to make fun of the whole proceeding, never doubting but that the sick man would enjoy the joke as much as he did. To his great surprise his friend turned from him in horror.

"Never speak to me in such a way

panion of his boyhood.
became a punishment to r
" and my father's house a
places or things in which I ha
with him were turned into a
to me, being now without
sought him everywhere, ar
things because they had l
thought of death was full of
and he gave way to a deep c
health, never very robust, be

Romanianus, much as he
him at Tagaste, realized th
scene would be the best thi
agreed to his proposal to ret
and open a school of rhetori
his other disciples followed

rush of the great city Augustine regained, to some extent, his peace of mind. While teaching, he continued his own studies, and competed for the public prizes. Many men of note joined his school, and his name began to be famous.

He greatly desired honour, he tells us, but only if honourably won. One day a certain magician paid him a visit. He had heard, he said, that Augustine was about to compete for one of the State prizes in rhetoric. What would he be ready to give if he could insure him the victory? It was only necessary to offer some living creatures in sacrifice to the demons whom he worshipped and success would be certain. Augustine turned from him in horror and disgust. He had not yet fallen so low as this.

"I would not sacrifice a fly," he retorted hotly, " to win a crown of gold!"

The magician retired in haste, and Augustine, who succeeded in carrying off the prize without the help of the demons, was publicly crowned by the Pro-Consul Vindicius, who from thenceforth joined the circle of his friends.

The news of his success reach
Her mother's heart rejoiced in h
but her joy was tempered wi
Carthage had taken more from h
it could ever give him, and her th
of other victories and other crow
his stay in Tagaste, although Au
not lived under the same roof with
he had been continually with her.
affection had been his greatest
the deep sorrow after his friend's
spoke no more to her of religio
mindful of the old Bishop's word
silent.

"While I was struggling in th
in the darkness of error," writes
"that holy, chaste, devout, and
(such as Thou lovest) ceased no
hours of her prayers to bewail me

thing in his soul that none of these things could satisfy. " After Thee, O Truth," he cries, " I hungered and thirsted !" His heart still ached for the loss of his friend, he turned everywhere for comfort and found none. He sought forgetfulness in study. He wrote two books on the " Beautiful " and the " Apt," and dedicated them to Hierus, a famous Roman orator. " It seemed to me a great thing," he tells us, " that my style and my studies should be known to such a man."

Monica drew fresh hope from her son's writings. They were full of noble thoughts and high aspirations. Such a mind could not remain in error. Some day, surely, in God's good time, he would come to know the truth.

HOW AUGUSTINE PLANNED TO GO TO ROM[E] AND HOW HE CRUELLY DECEIVED H[IS] MOTHER.

IT was about this time that Augustin[e's] enthusiasm for the Manicheans began to co[ol.] He had been studying their doctrines, a[nd] had found that they were not quite what [he] thought. He was disappointed with th[e] professors too.

The first unpleasant truth that dawn[ed] upon him was that they were much better [at] denying the doctrines of the Catholic Chur[ch] than at explaining their own. It was alm[ost] impossible to find out what they believed, [so] vague did they become when closely qu[es]tioned. And Augustine questioned ve[ry] closely indeed. He was on the track [of] truth, and it was not easy to put him

er step he wanted to be certain
id. The men whom he consult
eem very certain of their own,
ed, but they bade him have pa
of their bishops, Faustus by nar
coming to Carthage. He was
most brilliant preachers, and we
to answer all Augustine's questio
is sounded promising, and Au
ted his coming impatiently. I
y was an eloquent speaker; his s
charming. But when Augustin
m privately and explained his do
the result was not what he had
He gave the same vague answe
istine had so often heard a
cd closer, he frankly replied t
not learned enough to be a
y him. Augustine was pleased
sty, and they became good friend
seeker was no nearer the trut
e.

to be found there either. Was t
thing at all? was the final questi
himself. The old philosophers, :
they were, seemed to get nearer to
things than this.

Yet now and again, out of the v
of his soul, a prayer would break
Christ Whom he had known and
boyhood, but Who had grown so
since the Manicheans had taugh
His Sacred Humanity was not
shadow. He was weary of life,
of pleasure, weary of everything,
of all of Carthage.

Owing to the wild ways of the
was impossible to keep anything
in the schools. Classes were cons

rupted by gangs of " smashers," who might break in at any moment, setting the whole place in an uproar.

Augustine's friends pressed him to go to Rome. There, they urged, he would meet with the honour that he deserved. There the students were quieter and better-mannered; no rioting was allowed; scholars might enter no school but that of their own master. This sounded hopeful; Augustine was rather pleased with the idea. He wrote to Monica and to his patron Romanianus to tell them of the step he proposed to take.

Monica's heart sank when she read the letter. To the Christians of the fourth century Rome was another Babylon. She had poured out the blood of the saints like water; she was the home of every abomination. What would become of Augustine in Rome? Without faith, without ideals, a disabled ship, drifting with every wind.

He must not go, she decided, or if he did she would go with him. She prayed that she might be able to make him give up the project, and wrote strongly against it; but Augustine had already made up his mind.

Then, in despair, she set out for Carthage to make one last effort.

Her son was touched by her grief and her entreaties, but his plans were made: he was to start that very night. "I lied to my mother," he says, "and such a mother!" He assured her that he was not going, that she might set her mind at rest. A friend of his was leaving Carthage, and he had promised to go down to the harbour to see him off.

Some instinct warned Monica that he was deceiving her. "I will go with you," she said. This was very awkward for her son; he was at his wit's end to know what to do. They went down to the harbour together, where they found Augustine's friend. No ship could put out that night, the sailors said, the wind was dead against them. The young men were unwilling to leave the harbour in case the wind should change and they should miss the boat, while Monica was determined not to leave Augustine.

They walked up and down together on the seashore in the cool evening air. The hours passed, and the situation became more and more difficult for Augustine. What was he

THE CHAPEL ON THE SHORE 89

)? Monica was weary and worn out
grief. An idea suggested itself to him
nly. It was no use waiting any longer,
id, it would be better to take some
the boat would certainly not start that

nica was in no mood to rest; but Augus-
knew her love of prayer. There was a
chapel on the seashore, dedicated to
yprian. Would she not at least go
and take shelter until the morning?
romised her again that he would not
Carthage, and she at last consented,
er soul was full of sorrow.
eeling there in the stillness of the little
l, she poured out the troubles of her
to God, beseeching Him that He would
let Augustine leave her. The answer
d a strange one. As she prayed the
suddenly changed; the sailors prepared
part. Augustine and his friend went
ard, and the ship set sail for Rome.
e last thing they saw as the shore faded

lonely figure that stood on the sand and stretched out piteous hands to Heaven, wailing for the son whom she had lost a second time.

It was God alone Who knew all the bitterness of that mother's heart. It was God alone Who knew how, after the first uncontrollable outburst of grief, she bent herself in faith and love to endure the heartbreak—silent and uncomplaining. And it was only God Who knew that the parting that seemed so cruel was to lead to the granting of her life-long prayer, to be the first stage in her son's conversion.

"She turned herself to Thee to pray for me," says Augustine, "and went about her accustomed affairs, and I arrived at Rome."

It seemed, indeed, as if his arrival in Rome was destined to be the end of his earthly career, for soon afterwards he was attacked by a violent fever and lay at death's door. He was lodging in the house of a Manichean, for, although he no longer held with their doctrines, he had many friends among them in Carthage who had recommended him to some of their sect in Rome.

ST. AUGUSTINE DECEIVES HIS MOTHER AND SAILS AWAY TO ROME.

To face p. 90.

should be broken and her prayers un
swered. He recovered, and began to tea

Already while he was in Carthage he
suspected that the lives of the Manich
were not much better than those of
heathens among whom they lived, altho
they gave out that their creed was the
one likely to reform human nature. In R
his suspicions were confirmed. Thinking
Augustine was altogether one of themsel
they threw off the mask and showed th
selves in their true colours.

The pagans at least were honest. T
professed openly that they lived for noth
but enjoyment, and in this great city,
more than in Carthage, one could learn
low a man might fall; but at least they
not hypocrites. He resolved to cut hin
adrift from the Manicheans altogether.

There was a Christian Rome within
pagan Rome, but of this Augustine k

nothing. On the Throne of tl
sat St. Damasus, wise and holy
tary, St. Jerome, was already fa
for his eloquence than for the
his character. Jerome, like A1
been carried away in his youth
ward tide, but had retrieved
glorious penance. The descen
oldest Roman families were to
the hospitals tending the sick
amongst the poor in the great ci
monasteries were growing up, li1
faith and prayer in the desert
peopled by men and women who
the world well lost for Christ,
who to save their souls had fled
St. Benedict was to do later, 1
ruptions that had dragged down
the abyss.

Augustine had been great
shortly before leaving Carth
preaching of Helpidius, a Ca
The idea came to him while ir
to the Catholics and find ou
really taught. But he dismi

that no intelligent man could accept their doctrines. Besides, they were too strict; their ideals were too high; he would have to give up too much.

One more honest impulse was stifled. He entered a school of philosophers who professed to believe in nothing. It was, he decided, the wisest philosophy he knew.

CHAPTER IX

HOW AUGUSTINE CAME TO MILAN, AND HOW HIS TEMPEST-TOSSED SOUL FOUND LIGHT AND PEACE AT LAST

AUGUSTINE had not been a year in Rome before he discovered that the ways of the Roman students were not quite so delightful as he had been led to believe. They were less insolent, it is true, than those of Carthage, and not so rough; but they had other defects which were quite as trying. They would, for instance, attend the classes of a certain professor until the time arrived to pay their fees, when, deserting in a body to another school, they would proceed to play the same trick there. It was certainly one way of getting an education for nothing, but it was hard on the teachers. It seemed scarcely the profession in which one would be likely to make a fortune, even if it were possible to earn one's daily bread. Augustine was discouraged and sick at heart; everything seemed to be against him; there was no hope, no light anywhere. His life seemed doomed to be a failure, in spite of all his gifts.

And then, quite suddenly, came the opening that he had longed for. Symmachus, the Prefect of Rome, received a letter from Milan, requesting him to name a professor of rhetoric for the vacant chair in that city. A competition was announced in which Symmachus, himself a well-known orator, was to be the judge. Augustine entered and won the prize. It was an excellent and honourable position. The professor was supported by the State. The Emperor Valentinian held his Court in the city, which gave it a certain position.

Augustine was furnished with letters of introduction to Ambrose, the Bishop, who had been brilliantly successful at the Bar in his youth, and was probably an old friend of Symmachus. He was of a noble Roman family, and famous alike for his great learning and peculiar charm of manner. He was famous also for his holiness of life, but this was of less interest to Augustine; it was Ambrose the orator with whom he desired to make acquaintance.

No sooner had he arrived in Milan than he presented himself before the Bishop, who received him with a cordial courtesy that attracted Augustine at once. The only way to judge of his eloquence was to attend the sermons at the cathedral. This Augustine began to do regularly. He found that Ambrose had not been overpraised. He listened to him at first with the pleasure it always gave him to hear an eloquent speaker; then, gradually, with a shock of surprise, he began to attend to what the Bishop said, as well as to his manner of saying it.

Ambrose was explaining the doctrines of the Church. He spoke very clearly and simply, to the intelligence no less than to the heart, for there were many catechumens in his congregation, as well as pagans who were seeking for the truth.

The Manicheans had deceived him, then, thought Augustine; they had lied about the Church's teaching; or they themselves had been ignorant of it, and he had let himself

ed. This was altogether unlike
had told him. It was noble and
ll that was great and good in him
Had he found the Truth at last?
meantime Monica, determined to
;on, arrived in Milan. The journey
ong and dangerous; they had been
/ terrible storms; even the sailors
)urage. It was she who had com-
m in their fear. "The storm will
/er," she assured them; "I know
;hall reach our journey's end in
She had a strong conviction that
not die until her prayers had won
back to God. The sailors took
n at her words; her calm eyes
ed them; they felt that this gentle
ew things that were hidden from

first visit was to St. Ambrose.
)ble natures understood each other
'Thank God for having given you
her," said the Bishop to Augustine,
let him a few days later; "she is
10usand."

had parted, and much had to be told. The first thing that Monica heard was that Augustine had left the Manicheans. At this she rejoiced greatly; she was convinced, she told him, that she would see him a Catholic before she died. "Thus she spoke to me," says Augustine, "but to Thee, O Fountain of Mercy, she redoubled her prayers and her tears, beseeching Thee to hasten Thine aid and dispel my darkness." They went together now to the sermons and sat side by side in the Church as in the days of Augustine's childhood. One by one he laid aside the false ideas of the truth that had been given to him by the Manicheans. It was growing clearer to him every day. True, there was much that was above his understanding—above the understanding of any human being, as Ambrose frankly acknowledged—but not above their faith. The Manicheans had sneered at faith as childish and credulous; and yet, thought Augustine, how many things he believed that he could have no possibility of proving. He believed, for instance, that Hannibal had crossed the Alps, although he had not been present at ie. He believed that Athens existed, ;h he had never been there.

)f old, a little group of friends had :d round him at Milan. There was ;, the most beloved of all his asso- who had taken the place of the dear friend of his boyhood. There was ianus, who was there on State business, centius, his son, with Trigetius, both of Augustine's; Nebridius, who had /ith him in Carthage, and was, like , a native of Roman Africa; and new friends he had made in Milan. agreed amongst them that they should irt a certain time every day to seek truth, reading and discussing among lves. The Scriptures were to form the reading.

eat hope has dawned," wrote Augus- the Catholic Faith teaches not what ught and vainly accused it of. Life , death uncertain; if it steals upon us idden, in what state shall we depart
And where shall we learn what here

ST. MONICA

 ιere was in Milan a holy old priest
 ɔlicianus, greatly beloved by St.
 ϵ, for he had been his teacher and
 ɪrly life. To him Augustine resolv
 he might be able to help him. H
 ɔlicianus, amongst other things, th
 been reading a book of philosophy
 l by a Roman called Victorinus.
 ϲ was good, said Simplicianus, bu
 y of Victorinus' own life was better
 known him well in Rome. Aug
 interested; he would like to hea
 y, he said.
 ictorinus, said the old man, was a
 a worshipper of the heathen gods
 a famous orator, and taught rhetc
 ϵ of the noblest citizens of Rome
 learned in every science, and w
 ɔrated for his virtue that a statu
 ι erected to him in the forum.

ssion of faith aloud before the whole
egation, instead of making it, as was
, in private.

s courageous action of an old man
Augustine feel his own cowardice. He
ed now that the Catholic Church was
rue Church, and yet he could not face
nought of Baptism. He would have to
up so much. The Christian standard
nigh for a man who had spent his life
lf-indulgence. He could never attain
He took leave of Simplicianus sadly;
elp which he needed was not to be found

went about my usual business," he
" while my anxiety increased as I
sighed to Thee." He frequented the
ch now even when there were no sermons,
e began to feel the need of prayer.

e day when Alypius and he were alone
her there came in a friend of theirs,
tianus, a devout Christian, who held a
at the Emperor's Court. Finding the

teaching. He began to tell them about St. Anthony, and of the many hermitages and monasteries in Egypt, and even here in his own country. He spoke to them of the monastic life and its virtues, and, seeing their interest and astonishment, went on to tell them an incident that had happened a short time before.

Two young men of the Imperial Court, friends of his own, walking together in the country, came to a cottage inhabited by some holy recluses. A life of St. Anthony lay on the table. One of them took it up and began to read. His first feeling was one of astonishment, his second of admiration. "How uncertain life is!" he said suddenly to his companion. "We are in the Emperor's service. I wish we were in God's; I had rather be His friend than the Emperor's." He read on, with sighs and groans. At last he shut the book and arose. "My mind is made up," he said; "I shall enter God's service here and now. If you will not do so too, at least do not try to hinder me." "You have chosen well," said the other; "I am with you in this." They never left the hermitage.

A BITTER STRUGGLE 103

This story only increased Augustine's misery. He had had more graces than these young men, and had wasted them; he was a coward. When Pontitianus had gone away, he left Alypius and went out into the garden. Alypius followed and sat down beside him.

"What are we about!" cried Augustine hotly. "The unlearned take heaven by force, and we, with all our heartless learning, wallow in the mire!" He sank his face in his hands and groaned. The way lay clear before him; he had found the Eternal Truth for which he had been seeking so long, and he had not the courage to go further.

This and that he would have to do; this and that he would have to give up—he could not: it was too hard.

And yet—to stand with both feet on the rock of truth, was it not worth all this and more?

So the battle raged. Good and evil struggled together in his soul.

It seemed to him then that he saw a long procession winding across the garden. It passed him and faded in the distance. First boys and girls, young and weak, scarcely more than children, and they mocked him gently. "We have fought and conquered," they said, "even we." After them came a great multitude of men and women in the prime of life, some strong and vigorous, some feeble and sickly. It seemed to Augustine as if they looked at him with eyes full of contempt. "We have lived purely," they said, "we have striven and conquered." They were followed by old men and women, worn with age and suffering. They looked at him reproachfully. "We have fought and conquered," they said, "we have entered unto the end."

Augustine's self-control was leaving him; even Alypius' presence was more than he could bear. He leapt to his feet, went to the other end of the garden, and, throwing himself down on the ground, wept as if his heart would break. His soul, tossed this way and that in its anguish, cried desperately to

lege; tolle, lege," rang the sweet voice aga and again in his ear, now on this sid now on that. Was this the answer to l prayer?

He remembered how St. Anthony h opened the sacred Scriptures on a like occ sion, and had found the help that he require Going back to Alypius, he took up the sacr volume and opened it. " Put ye on t Lord Jesus Christ, and make not provisi for the flesh and the concupiscence thereof he read.

Light, strength, and conviction flowed in his soul. With God's help all things we possible; he would give up all and follo Him. Then, having carefully marked t place, he sat down beside Alypius and to him of his resolution.

" What about me?" asked Alypius. " P haps there is something there for me to Let me see." He took the book from Augu tine, opened at the place he had mark and read: " He that is weak in the faith ta unto you." "That will do very well for me," he said.

Augustine's first thought was for Monica. He must go to her, and at once. They sat together hand in hand until the sun sank in a rose-coloured glory and the cool shadows of the evening fell like a blessing on the earth. There are some joys too deep for speech, too holy to be touched by mortal hands.

CHAPTER X

HOW ST. MONICA LIVED AT CASSIACUM WITH AUGUSTINE AND HIS FRIENDS, AND HOW AUGUSTINE WAS BAPTIZED BY ST. AMBROSE

AMONGST the saints there are two great penitents, St. Mary Magdalene and St. Augustine, who in the first moment of their conversion shook themselves wholly free from the trammels of the past and never looked back again.

"Thou hast broken my bonds in sunder," cries St. Augustine, "to Thee will I offer the sacrifice of praise." Honours, wealth, pleasure, all the things he had desired so passionately, were now as nothing to him. "For Thou didst expel them from me," he says, "and didst come in Thyself instead of them. And I sang to Thee, my Lord God, my true honour, my riches, and my salvation."

The vacation was close at hand. Augustine resolved to give up his professorship and to go away quietly to prepare himself for Baptism. Verecundus, one of the little group of faithful friends who surrounded him, had a country house in Cassiacum, which he offered for his use while he remained in Italy. It was a happy party that gathered within its walls. There were Augustine and his younger brother Navigius; the faithful Alypius, who was to receive Baptism with his friend; Licentius and Trigetius, Augustine's two pupils; and several others. Lastly there was Monica, who was a mother to them all, and whose sunny presence did much to enliven the household. It was autumn, an Italian mid-September. The country was a glory of green and gold and crimson, the Apennines lying like purple shadows in the distance.

Here, in the seclusion that was so dear to his heart, Augustine read the Psalms for the first time. His soul was on fire with their beauty; every word carried him to God. Monica read with him, and he tells us that he would often turn to her for an explanation. "For," he continues, "she was walking steadily in the path in which I was as yet feeling my way."

There were other studies besides to be carried on, and St. Augustine tells us of some of the interesting discussions that were held on the lawn, or in the hall of the baths, which they used when the weather was not fine enough to go out.

One morning, when he and his pupils were talking of the wonderful harmony and order that exist in nature, the door opened and Monica looked in.

"How are you getting on?" she asked, for she knew what they were discussing. Augustine invited her to join them, but Monica smiled. "I have never heard of a woman amongst the philosophers," she said.

"That is a mistake," replied Augustine. "There were women philosophers amongst the ancients, and you know, my dear mother, that I like your philosophy very much. Philosophy means nothing else but love of wisdom. Now you love wisdom more even than you love me, and I know how much that is. Why, you are so far advanced in wisdom that you fear no ill-fortune, not even death itself. Everybody says that this is the very height of philosophy. I will therefore sit at your feet as your disciple."

Monica, still smiling, told her son that he had never told so many lies in his life. In spite of her protests, however, they would not let her go, and she was enrolled amongst the philosophers. The discussions, says St. Augustine, owed a good deal of their beauty to her presence.

The 15th of November was Augustine's birthday. After dinner he invited his friends to come to the hall of the baths, that their souls might be fed also.

"For I suppose you all admit," he said, when they had settled themselves for conversation, "that we are made up of soul and body." To this everybody agreed but Navigius, who was inclined to argue, and who said he did not know.

"Do you mean," asked Augustine, "that there is nothing at all that you do know, or that of the few things you do not know this is one?"

Navigius was a little put out at this question, but they pacified him, and at last per-

:d him to say that he was as certain of
act that he was made up of body and
ıs anybody could be. They then agreed
food was taken for the sake of the body.
lust not the soul have its food too?"
l Augustine. "And what is that food?
not knowledge?"

nica agreed to this, but Trigetius ob-
l.

Vhy, you yourself," said Monica, " are
ng proof of it. Did you not tell us at
r that you did not know what you were
g because you were lost in thought?
your teeth were working all the time.
e was your soul at that moment if not
ıg too?"

en Augustine, reminding them that it

tion. "If he wants what is good and has i she replied, "he is happy. But if he wa: what is bad, he is not happy even if he has it

"Well said, mother!" cried Augusti "You have reached the heights of philosop at a single bound."

Someone then said that if a man w needy he could not be happy. Finally th all agreed that only he who possessed G could be wholly happy. But the discussi had gone on for a long time, and August suggested that the soul might have too mu nourishment as well as the body, and th it would be better to put off the rest ur to-morrow.

The discussion was continued next day.

"Since only he who possesses God can happy, who is he who possesses God?" asl Augustine, and they were all invited to g their opinion.

"He that leads a good life," answered o

St. Augustine continued: " It is God's will that all should seek Him ? "

" Of course," they all replied.

" Can he who seeks God be leading a bad life ? "

" Certainly not," they said.

" Can a man who is not pure in heart seek God ? "

" No," they agreed.

" Then," said Augustine, " what have we here ? A man who leads a good life, does God's will, and is pure of heart, is seeking God. But he does not yet possess Him. Therefore we cannot uphold that they who lead good lives, do God's will, and are pure of heart, possess God."

They all laughed at the trap in which he had caught them. But Monica, saying that she was slow to grasp these things, asked to have the argument repeated. Then she thought a moment.

" No one can possess God without seeking Him," she said.

" True," said Augustine, " but while he is seeking he does not yet possess."

" I think there is no one who does not have

God," she said. "But those who live well have Him for their friend, and those who live badly make themselves His enemies. Let us change the statement, 'He who possesses God is happy' to 'He who has God for his friend is happy.'"

All agreed to this but Navigius.

"No," he said, "for this reason. If he is happy who has God for his friend (and God is the friend of those who seek Him, and those who seek Him do not possess Him, for to this all have agreed), then it is obvious that those who are seeking God have not what they want. And we all agreed yesterday that a man cannot be happy unless he has what he wants."

Monica could not see her way out of this difficulty, although she was sure there was one. "I yield," she said, "for logic is against me."

"Well," said Augustine, "we have reached the conclusion that he who has found God has Him for his friend and is happy; but he who is still seeking God has Him for his

has neither God for his friend nor is he happy."

This satisfied everybody.

The other side of the question was then considered.

"In what did unhappiness consist?" asked Augustine.

Monica maintained that neediness and unhappiness must go together. "For he who has not what he wants," she said, "is both needy and unhappy."

Augustine then supposed a man who had everything he wanted in this world. Could it be said that he was needy? Yet was it certain that he was happy?

Licentius suggested that there would remain with him the fear of losing what he had.

"That fear," replied Augustine, "would make him unhappy but would not make him needy. Therefore we could have **a man** who is unhappy without being needy."

To this everyone agreed but Monica, who still argued that unhappiness could **not be** separated from neediness.

"This supposed man of yours," she said, "rich and fortunate, still fears to lose his good fortune. That shows that he wants wisdom. Can we call a man who wants money needy, and not call him so when he wants wisdom?"

At this remark there was a general outcry of admiration. It was the very argument, said Augustine, that he had meant to use himself.

"Nothing," said Licentius, "could have been more truly and divinely said. What, indeed, is more wretched than to lack wisdom? And the wise man can never be needy, whatever else he lacks."

Augustine then went on to define wisdom. "The wisdom that makes us happy," he said, "is the wisdom of God, and the wisdom of God is the Son of God. Perfect life is the only happy life," he continued, "and to this, by means of firm faith, cheerful hope, and burning love we shall surely be brought if we but hasten towards it."

So the discussion ended, and all were content.

"Oh," cried Trigetius, "how I wish you would provide us with a feast like this every day!"

"Moderation in all things," answered Augustine. "If this has been a pleasure to you, it is God alone that you must thank."

So the happy innocent days flew past in the pursuit of that wisdom which is eternal. "Too late have I loved Thee, O Beauty ever ancient, ever new!" cried Augustine. "Behold Thou wast within me, and I was abroad, and there I sought Thee. I have tasted Thee, and I am hungry after Thee. Thou hast touched me, and I am all on fire."

At the beginning of Lent Augustine and Alypius returned to Milan to attend the course of instructions which St. Ambrose was to give to those who were preparing for Baptism.

In the night between Holy Saturday and Easter Sunday the stains of the past were washed away for ever in those cleansing waters, and at the Mass of the daybreak on that blessed morning Augustine knelt at the altar to receive his Lord. Monica was beside him; her tears and her prayers had been answered. She and her son were one again in heart and soul.

CHAPTER XI

MONICA SET OUT FOR AFRICA WITH [A]UGUSTINE, AND HOW SHE DIED AT [A] ON THE TIBER

[In his last] days at Milan, before his conversion, [h]e had often told his friends that the [dream of] his life was to live quietly some[where] wi[th] a few friends, who would devote [themselves] to the search for truth. It had [been] proposed to try the scheme, but [it would] not work. Some of his friends [were mar]ried; others had worldly ties that [they coul]d not break. The idea had to be

[Now he] had found the Truth, and at Cas-

should they live this life but in their own country, which was to be the future field of their labours?

Alypius asked nothing better. Their friend Evodius, like themselves a citizen of Tagaste, who had been baptized a short time before, was ready to join them. He held a high position at the Court of the Emperor, but it seemed to him a nobler thing to serve the King of kings. So these three future bishops of the Church in Africa made their plans together. Monica would be the mother of the little household, as she had been at Cassiacum; she was ready to go wherever they wished.

A few days before they started an event occurred which they all remembered later. It was the feast of St. Cyprian, and Monica had returned from Mass absorbed in God, as she always was after Holy Communion. Perhaps she had been thinking of her night of anguish in the little chapel by the seashore at Carthage three years before, when God had seemed deaf to her prayers, in order that He might grant her the fulness of her heart's desire.

:t us hasten to heaven!" she cried.
y gently questioned her as to w
:ant, but she did not seem to hear th(
soul and my flesh have rejoiced in
God," she said, and they marvelled
avenly beauty of her face.

'as a long journey from Milan to O:
e Tiber, where they were to set
rica. They remained there for sc
for the ship was not to start at on(
evening Augustine and Monica w
together at a window that overlool
.rden and the sea. They were talk
ven, St. Augustine tells us, asking e:
what that eternal life of the sai
be which eye hath not seen nor
How small in comparison were
of earth, they said, even the m
ful of God's creations; for all th
were less than He who made th(
eir two souls stretched out toget
Is the infinite Love and Wisdom,
1 to them that for one moment, w
:at of the heart, they touched It, ;

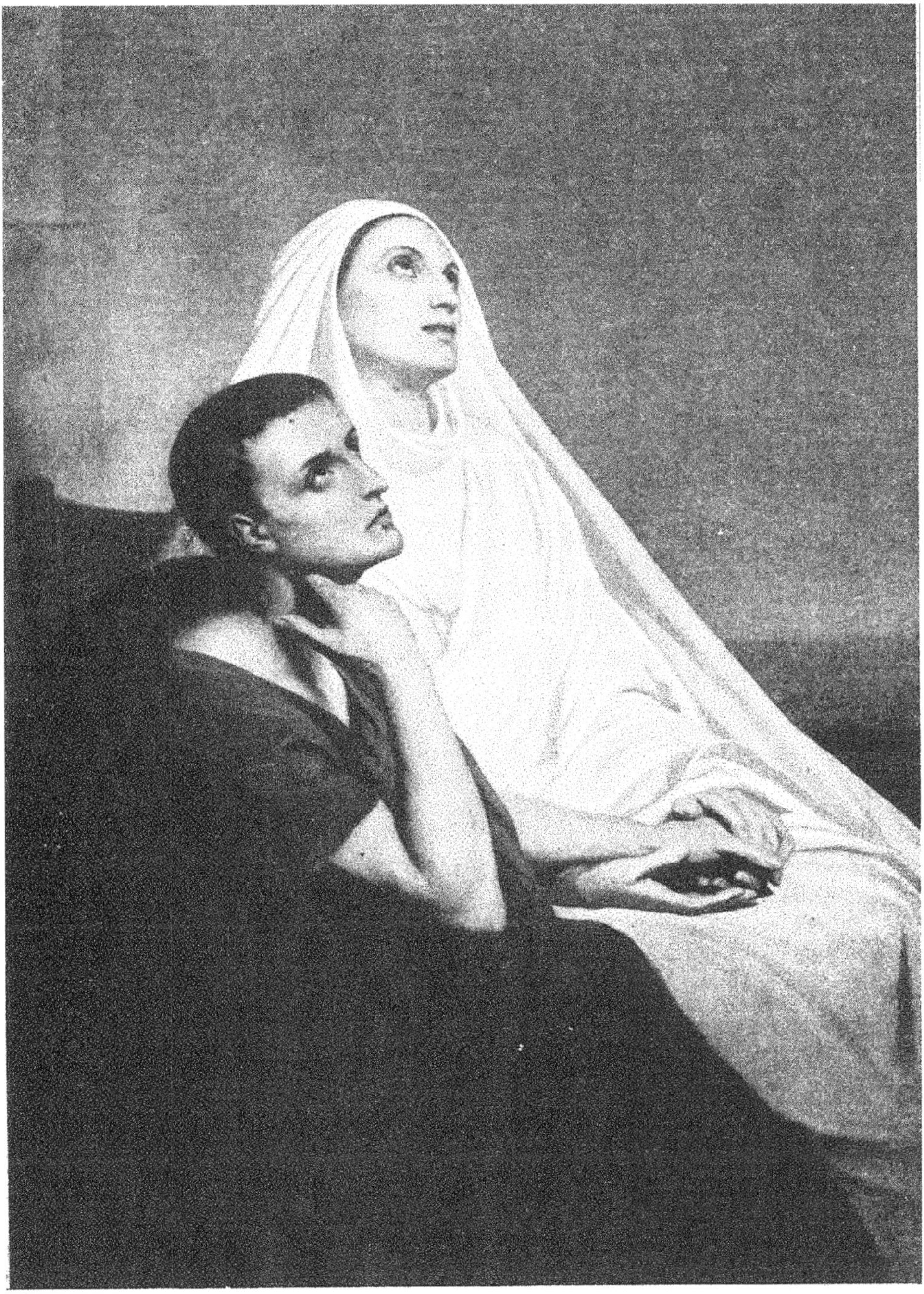

WHAT HAVE I TO LIVE FOR?

the joy of that moment was a foreshadowing of eternity.

They sighed as it faded from them, and they were forced to return again to the things of earth.

"Son," said Monica, "there is nothing in this world now that gives me any delight. What have I to do here any longer? I know not, for all I desired is granted. There was only one thing for which I wished to live, and that was to see you a Christian and a Catholic before I died. And God has given me even more than I asked, for He has made you one of His servants, and you now desire no earthly happiness. What am I doing here?"

About five days afterwards she fell ill of a fever. They thought she was tired with the long journey, and would soon be better; but she grew worse, and was soon unconscious. When she opened her eyes, Augustine and Navigius were watching by her bed.

"You will bury your mother here," she said. Augustine could not trust himself to speak; but Navigius, who knew how great had been her desire to be buried at Tagaste

ST. MONICA

her husband, protested. "Oh, why
 not at home," he cried, "where you
wish to be!" Monica looked at him
chfully. "Do you hear what he says?"
ked Augustine. "Lay my body any-
" she said; "it does not matter. Do
 that disturb you. This only I ask—
you remember me at God's Altar
ver you may be."
ie is never far from God," she answered
ther person who asked her if it would
 a sorrow to her to be buried in a land
from home.
as not only her sons who grieved, but
ithful friends who were with them, for
ie not their mother too? Had she not
as much care of them as if they had
ier children?

My life was torn in two," says Augustine. at life which was made up of mine and

ey were all with her when she passed efully away a few days later. They ed back their tears. " It did not seem ," says Augustine, " to celebrate that with groans and lamentations. Such s were fit for a less blessed deathbed, not for hers."

en, as they knelt gazing at the beloved that seemed to be smiling at some unmystery, Evodius had a happy intion. Taking up the Psalter, he opened the 110th Psalm.

will praise Thee, O Lord, with my e heart," he sang softly, " in the assembly e just and in the congregation."

Great are the works of the Lord," sang others, with trembling voices, " sought as they are according unto all His sure." Friends and religious women who gathered near the house to pray entered joined in the chant. It was the voice that pure soul on its way to heaven. e alone was silent, for his heart was

 but human, after all, and the sense loss fell upon them all later. That ıgustine lay thinking of his mother's the unselfish love of which it had full. " Thy handmaid, so pious Thee, so careful and tender towards I I let go my tears," he tells us, t them flow as much as they would. for her, who for so many years had me."
buried her, as she herself had fore- Ostia, where her sacred relics were a thousand years later by Pope V., and carried to the Church of ıstine in Rome.
nemory of the mother to whom he much remained with Augustine until of his death. He loved to speak of ıirty years later, while preaching to le at Hippo, he said:
dead do not come back to us. If it , how often should I see my holy

ND - #0013 - 250822 - C0 - 229/152/7 [9] - CB - 9781528560757 - Gloss Lamination